Out in the Open

Out in the Open

Life on the Street

Photographs by Bob Ballantyne

Northstone

Editor: Michael Schwartzentruber

Cover design: Lois Huey-Heck and Margaret Kyle

Interior design: Margaret Kyle

Consulting art director: Robert MacDonald

Northstone Publishing Inc. is an employee-owned company, committed to caring for the environment and all creation. Northstone recycles, reuses and composts, and encourages readers to do the same. Resources are printed on recycled paper and more environmentally friendly groundwood papers (newsprint), whenever possible. The trees used are replaced through donations to the Scoutrees For Canada Program. Ten percent of all profit is donated to charitable organizations.

Canadian Cataloguing in Publication Data

Ballantyne, Bob, 1947-
  Out in the Open

ISBN 1-55145-099-2

1. Homeless persons — Pictorial works. 2. Urban poor — Pictorial works. 3. Homeless persons' writings. I. Title.
HV4493.B34 1996   305.5'69   C96-910691-2

Published by Northstone Publishing Inc.

Northstone

Printed in Canada by Friesens Printing

Dedication

This book was inspired and initiated by the men and women of the street.
Many have died since we began. The book is dedicated to their memory.

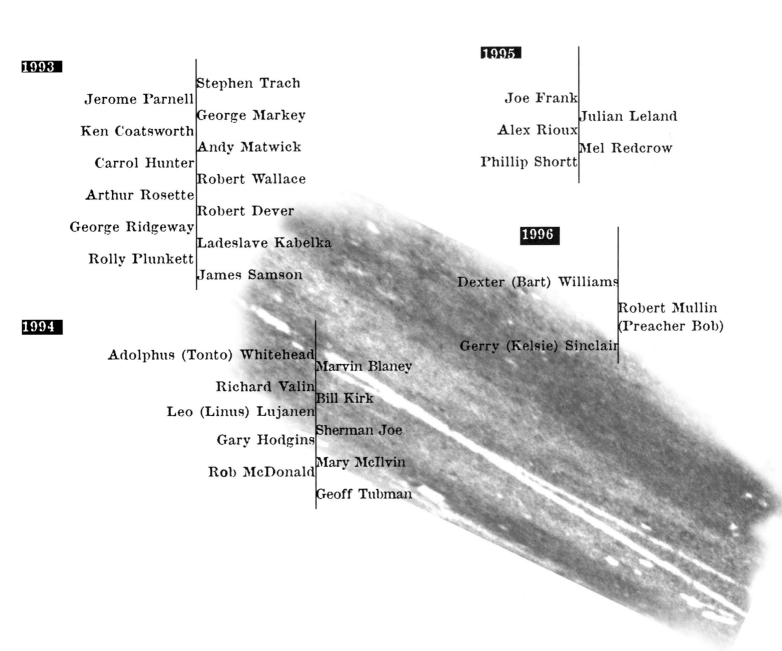

1993

Stephen Trach
Jerome Parnell
George Markey
Ken Coatsworth
Andy Matwick
Carrol Hunter
Robert Wallace
Arthur Rosette
Robert Dever
George Ridgeway
Ladeslave Kabelka
Rolly Plunkett
James Samson

1994

Adolphus (Tonto) Whitehead
Marvin Blaney
Richard Valin
Bill Kirk
Leo (Linus) Lujanen
Sherman Joe
Gary Hodgins
Rob McDonald
Mary McIlvin
Geoff Tubman

1995

Joe Frank
Julian Leland
Alex Rioux
Mel Redcrow
Phillip Shortt

1996

Dexter (Bart) Williams
Robert Mullin (Preacher Bob)
Gerry (Kelsie) Sinclair

Robert (Rockie) DeYoung

The life stories of the street are as varied and many as the men and women themselves. On the street you will find stories from the very rich to the very poor, from the very young to the very elderly, from the uneducated to the Harvard professor. You will find stories of failure, stories of oppression, stories of death, stories of joy and laughter, stories of the day-to-day struggle with life itself. You see, poverty has no boundaries; the old saying "There but by the grace of God go I" stands as a statement of fact. One story is no more important than any other story.

Preface

It is a pleasure and honor to have been invited by men and women who know the streets to be their home to write this preface. I am a minister of the church. God's call to ministry has led me outside the walls of the church, to the street, to the men and women who live out daily the reality of this book.

This book is a gift to you who are brave enough not only to open its pages, but to reach into its very soul and partake of its treasures. It is offered both as a challenge and an opportunity for the reader to move beyond their limited frame of reference. It is offered, not from the board rooms of the powerful, but from the back alleys amid the stench of poverty. It is a gift from the grass roots; it is a gift from God's people.

The people within these pages know themselves. It is their hope that with this gift you will be challenged to know them as well. If you engage yourself in that challenge, then within these pages you will have the opportunity to find yourself. The essence of this book is not the many questions, assumptions, and myths that surround poverty; rather the essence is the challenge and opportunity to question oneself.

This book is not an attempt to justify, glorify, or romanticize life on the street, nor is it an attempt to seek your forgiveness, compassion, or understanding. It is a gift of love and self-sacrifice simply given to you. This book was conceived in a back alley amid the garbage and filth as a bottle of mouthwash was being passed from one person to the next. Some of the people who were present to witness the birth of this project have since died; Jim Samson, Art Rosette, Adolphus Whitehead and others now fly with the eagles. Their street deaths did not end the project. It was their struggle with the street, their dedication and their passionate belief that this book would be completed and published, that has time and time again resurrected these pages.

Open the pages of your gift. It is yours to do with as you choose.

Rev. Allen Tysick

Jack James Jr.

We are a proud people.

We are a lonely people.

Let me tell you
something;
You do not really know us

and you do not wish to
                              know us,

for in us you will find
yourself!

Lisa Louie

Brothers and Sisters
Sun and Moon:
No mountains to climb,
 some of us build our   own.

One doesn't need to be in prison
 to be imprisoned –
some of us build our own.

But beyond the barriers, my friend,
I am not the only one with tears.
    Tears come not only to the poor,
but to the rich and powerful too.

But if my tears could paint a picture,
    they would   paint a rainbow,
the sun would shine all day,
and from what's left
I wish happiness
                for me and   for you.

Rocky

You wake up and smell the flowers.

We wake up in the flowers
and smell ourselves
and drink so that we don't
                        have to.

Ritchie

I would not change my life.

I am who I am.

I have accepted that.
I believe that God
            has   accepted
                     me
                        also.

Barbara Schreck

Human Portrait

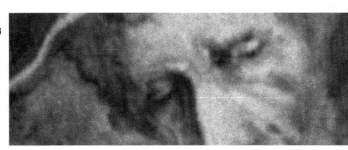

A strange mosaic of equal parts creates
the
    human portrait.
To negate the value of the blending
is but vain conceit.
A potential masterpiece cannot evolve
w i t h o u t   r e s p e c t.
When one life has been discounted,
no life can be complete.
How many lives are yet to be sacrificed on the
altar of indifference?
How many silent cries for help
violently denied?
The ultimate tragedy and shame
is not death, but how a people dies.
A search for meaning in the sacrifice,
deliverance from the pain,
finds but a cold, uncaring epitaph
that screams denial of the blame.

Robert
McGowan

searching for the Seeds

Walking down the miles within my mind –

empty.

Going down the road – unseeing.
Unbelieving in a dream,
embalmed damn near, consumed,
devoid, entrapped, enraged,
entombed.

Now standing here alone unjudged;

now leaving unperceived.

Alone again
on nights such as these,
creating, pretending my mind is appeased.
The dawns I've spent
walking through the late summer's breeze,
trying to cultivate my meaning
and
searching for the seeds.

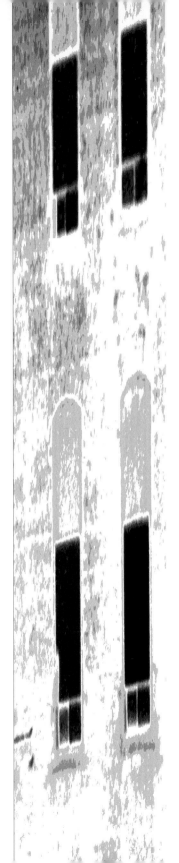

Gillis

My friend Andre was panning on the street one day. This elderly lady approached him and said, "You know, they said on television that you guys make a hundred dollars a day, each." Not about to let that slip by, he questioned, "So you believe everything you are told on TV?" She replied, "Well, yes I do, as a matter of fact." All he had left to say was, "So then you honestly believe that California raisins sing and dance?"

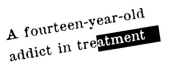

A Fish Story

When a trout rising to a fly gets hooked
on a line and finds himself unable to
swim freely, he begins a fight which
results in struggles and splashes and
sometimes an escape. Often, of course,
the situation is too tough for him.

In the same way, the human being
struggles with the hooks that catch him.
Sometimes he masters his difficulties.
Sometimes they are too tough for him.
His struggle is all that the world sees and
it naturally misunderstands him.

It is hard for a free fish to
understand what is happening
to a hooked one.

Kel sie

I am a native American
but I was raised
by a white family.
I was rejected by both
cultures.
I only found a sense of
family working the carnies
and living on the streets.

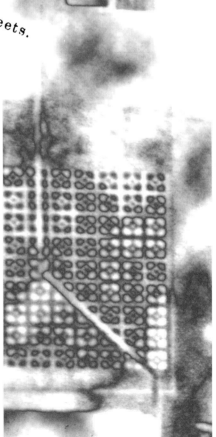

Ellenor

So much ignorance.
So many people
who just don't care.
It frustrates me.
They only like
the beauty of you.
The best of you.
So many sickening thoughts
in this world.
They all walk by
and laugh at you.
Like you're a joke –
like you're nothing.

Pat
McCleary

Loneliness ~ Despair

Drives me to drink.
Alcohol is an instant cure
and a few good drinks in the morning,
a few laughs,
take away the pain.

The fear of being beaten to death
or of being disfigured
is far less than the desperate fear
of feeling alone,
with no way out.

Few of us do
get out of this tailspin.
Once I do, though,
I feel a need to return to the street,
to my friends and enemies.
It's a way of life – lonely as it is.

Loneliness is the killer.
Almost all of the people
that I've had the opportunity to meet
are smart, caring, talented people.
All with pain, losses, emptiness,
and little real emotion.

For most of us, though,
        loneliness and alcoholism
have won the battle.

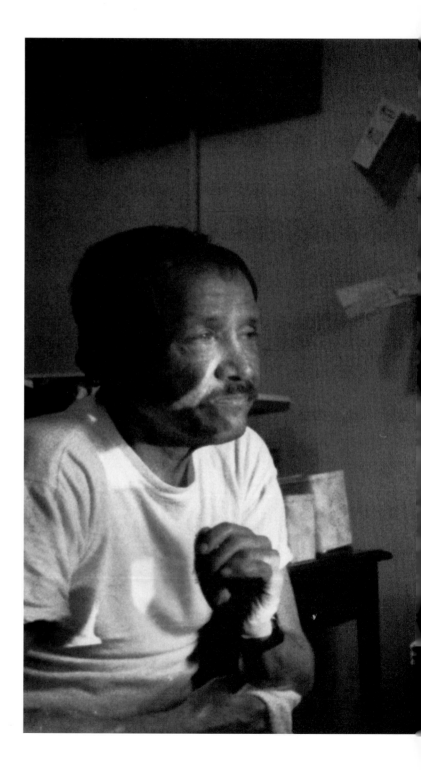

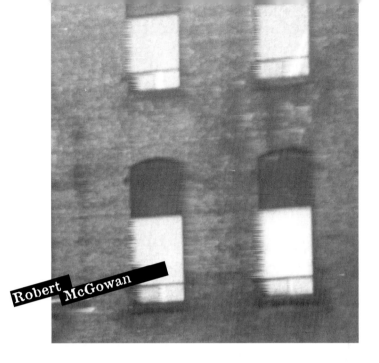

Robert McGowan

And all these things shall come to pass
                and little can be done,
but bend our backs and strive to do
before all time is gone.
We've all perceived,
through reddened eyes,
the turning of the tides,
  as if a place remained to stand,
above all waters rise.
Now standing in illusion,
so involved with what we "have,"
 we cannot bear to realize

these things that come to pass.

Howie
(China)

I think it's funny.

I get a good laugh

from hanging around the crew
because they make me laugh.
They're down —
so am I —
but together we are happy.

Robert McGowan

Words can but connote
the feelings which are better left unspoken
between us
and within the time we pass together
on the pathway from darkness unto light.
As day and night are separate,
so are we.
The breeze seems gentle,
yet a maelstrom has been prophesied and,
as if summoned,
promptly comes.
It seems futile now to bury one's head
in sand or stone,
as this distemper rages on
and widens the gap
between our collective delusions and
the separate realities we now face.

Still, hope, gusting, forms drifts of riddles,
and I stand alone
on the very pathway
where we once walked and spoke.
The road remains, as ever,
yet to be traversed.
For living in our dreams, and in the lies
that we conceived,
as makers of the games we played,
and masters of the wars we waged,
all we wrought has been brought down,
and will come crashing now

around any who would dwell within,
refusing to withdraw, even as the joists
crack.
Not a second more to waste!
Go down that road and bury the dead
with seed!
Repay what's owed! Right what's wrong!
Rebuild a more suitable
structure on a more solid foundation.
For it has been revealed to me
that if we could but all agree
on this one small
point,
this holocaust is past,
it will be done.

So, as was, is,
though time has seen all changed.
Most are altered, few remain the same,
and some will never be again.
This rain brings back warm memories...
laughing there, we stood half-soaked beneath the
street's light,
or perhaps the moon's glow.

Standing now, suddenly caught up
between then and now,
with no particular direction to go...
prophetically, you wrote our names together in
the melting snow.
Now, mostly for your safety's sake,
I'll travel light
and alone.

Rock**ie**

The truth is always best. The only trouble is — what is the truth?

Ritchie

There I lie in my own blood and vomit,
unconscious of the pain.
Awaiting the sting of death,
  to go home.

Then you picked me up –
took me to the hospital.
There the doctors and nurses

    brought me back to life.

You bastards!!

ara

Really
deep down
inside
I am a Teddy
Bear –
stuffed with
b r o k e n
glass.

Brenda Lynn

I want people
to know us
(street people)
as having
heart.

JoJo and
Baby Girl

We share our lives,
our pain,
our tears for those who lose.
   That's our reality —
the cold facts.
We also share our laughter
and our good times.
We might fight amongst ourselves,
but it means nothing.
Tomorrow it's forgotten.
In the crunch
we stand together.
The real truth is that we share from
our hearts —
not just on the surface,
but deep
down.

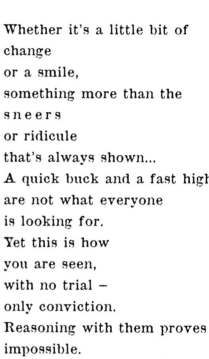

Isis

Whether it's a little bit of
change
or a smile,
something more than the
s n e e r s
or ridicule
that's always shown...
A quick buck and a fast high
are not what everyone
is looking for.
Yet this is how
you are seen,
with no trial —
only conviction.
Reasoning with them proves
impossible.
No one is trying
to hand you a pity trip.
Just trying to survive
in this very
judgmental world.

Mary **Miller**

Cocaine is my abusive lover.
It drives me to Hell,
and brings me to utopia.
I yearn for it,
I would kill for it.
And yet,
I feel the grip of cold
Death
upon me when I use it.

A er

I fall asleep dreaming of things that could be
only to wake up
   to the things that are real.
I wish there were only d r e a m s

      and nothing real.

Jo Jo

Reality sucks!

I've lost too much –
   my children,
my husband,
        my closest friend.

What do I
have to live for?

     I just wait
       for my time
       to come up.

Robert McGowan

Almost a nomad
he knew of his fate,
and ran toward the sunset
away from his hate.

Beyond reddened waters
the freedom he sought,
behind him the shadow
of fear he had wrought.

Cultivating dreams
 in a forest of weeds,
he went down on the dead
dust
of ungerminated s e e d s .

He went down
with no final word —
an unborn child,
u n s e e n, u n h e a r d...

The street,
cold and wet with snow,
his last vision,
what a way to go.

Slandered,
he'd been thought a fool
who would not
understand their rules.

He went down.
Had no lasting stay.
Some force refused
to guide his way.

Lying
in the yellowed snow,
out of his mind
he died alone.

Linda Jim

We are a family!
I wish people could see that we are
human —
we bleed, we cry, we suffer.
I wish people
could see that.

Rebel

People are
kind.
   This lady
saw me
begging
and brought
me two big
hamburgers
and a
milkshake,
but what
broke my
heart
was her
little girl
offering me
her coat.

Ritchie

Look on the
bright side;
the sun is
shining
and I'm not

in jail.

John

So You Think This Is Easy

So   you think this is easy,
 waking up on the cement at 3 a.m.,
the flop house is full again,
and you don't know where your kids are.

So you think this is easy,
 waking up to the news
that another brother is dead.

So you think this is easy,
 waking up to a sister sobbing,
her old man in jail,
no food in the house and the rent is due.

So you think this is easy,
 asking for money from people
with disdain in their eyes,
so you can have one more meal in your belly.

So you think this is easy.
 Come with me for one day
and see the life I choose,
then say this is e a s y .

Lois

In my world
there is beauty and peace.
There is no pain —
only love.

Then I

wake up.

Art

Life sucks –
who cares about me
  or you?
The streets are
my escape
from the reality of
  the bullshit that
is around me.
Open your eyes
  for Christ's sake.
That's what He wants
  you to do.
Just open your eyes.
The bullshit is up to
  our necks.

A Street Kid

They tell me
I can be
anything
I want to be.
They tell me
the world
is mine
and I tell them
I am
somebody.
I am a street
p e r s o n .

Art

"et tu, Brute?"
Shakespeare must have known the street
when he wrote that line.
Let's face it.
We all know our best friend
  might roll us this day for the bottle.
But w o r s e than that,
with each drink, each pill,
    each needle, and each bottle,
  the Brutus inside each of us

      pushes the knife of death deeper.

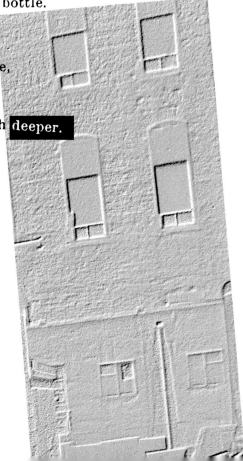

Rebel

Look at the trees —
 they change color,
the winds of the north blow,
winter is in the air.

 You know,
I do not believe
I will make it
through another winter.
I feel death is
k n o c k i n g
 on my door.

Look beyond what you see.
Look beyond what we are
  at the moment.
Look past our appearances and
smell.
Look into our souls
and there,
    there alone,
you will find the
                beauty
  you missed.

Paul Burnside

Every war has its casualties.
 Some return with
perfect bodies
but with huge scars on
    their psyche.
Some get medals.
Some get rewards.
Some get pensions.
Some are ignored
 and forgotten.
The statue of the
unknown soldier
 is for them.

The streets are no different.
Some have worked in mines,
some in the woods,
some in workshops,
some in factories,
some in offices.
Some had families –
 wives, husbands, children.
 We all forget that they
have produced and given
something special to all of us.

Sixpack

People look at us and think,

"What a pity, at least I'm not one of them."
Well first,
they do not understand our freedom,
our liberation from the rat race of society,
and second,
we do not want them to be one of   us anyway.

Rebel

If I could live my life over,
what would I like to be?

A wealthy drunk!

Stella

I cried to be heard.
I cried to be seen.
I cried for understanding.
I cried for love, and I am still crying.
No one can hear me for I am crying

      i n s i d e .

Bunny

Living on the   street
is like being lost in a m a z e.
You wander on and on,
but always end up where you began.
Like a lonely e c h O .

 Tracy
Yarel

You have seen the sunrise
    in the morning.
    You have tasted the dusty
    roadside soil.
You have been to places
    that no one has really seen.
    You have ridden
    with the wind and rain,
    and always

        you will be free.

TaMMy

There is no one
who would change places with me,
and there is no one
to take me out of the place I am at —
my world of make-believe.

Lisa

Louie

for Art

As I go on in my journey,

I cannot mourn.

Nor can I cry "tears of sadness,"

for you'll be looking down,

and my mind reflecting back,

to the great times I shared with you,

another "great spirit,"

who sits now with the Greatest Spirit of all.

Also,

the seasons will go on;

so must I.

But in my heart, s o u l, and s p i r i t

you,

m y   f r i e n d,

have not died —

just gone on to a better place

where the sweet winds

sing magical, mystical songs,

as the song in my heart will

be sung for you.

The seasons' winds will whisper your name

from time to time.

For you shall always remain

the same —

for your immortal soul

is no longer walking this plane.

But you are walking with the

U n f o r g o t t e n.

Jim Samson

The streets
are hard –

d   a   m   n

h a r d !

Mary
Miller

I have hurt you
(friends, family, loved ones).
I have used you.
I have forgotten you.
I have blamed you.

I have gone to jail —
to detox —
to long-term treatment.
Not once, not twice,
but time and time again,
one year following another.

But, alas, drugs are
my only r e l e a s e .
I'm not to blame.
You are not to blame.

I am sick.
This substance that I inject into my
body,
any way I can,
as often as I can,
as much as I can,
is in control.

It is like a fire burning
inside me,
consuming all that I am.
It is like a cancer that the doctors
and specialists
have given up on.

In death, God will crucify
the sickness.
And in death,
only then,
will I find rest
in G o d ' s   b o s o m .

Anonymous

I was drinking with this guy
whom I had seen before –
whom I didn't really trust,
but who had something about him
that attracted me to him.
It was a cold, wet night, and I was
really cold to the bone.
I noticed he didn't seem cold
although he wore fewer clothes than I.
I thought it was the booze,
but I asked him
and he said it was **love**
that kept him warm.
I realized then I didn't have that –
but I knew I needed it to stay alive.

Robert
McGowan

Give it a song
for the thoughts left
 unspoken.
Give it a tune
for those unwritten words.
Give it a meaning
for those who can
                    feel it.
Give it a voice
that will dare to be heard.
Give it to the ones
who foresaw our undoing.
Aim it at those
who still dwell in the past.
Give it a name
so that none can forget it.
Scratch it in stone
to go down with the last.
Leave it alone
not to touch and destroy it.
Revive it.
Remind them it's not
                    obsolete.

Live and believe it
so none can deny it.
And sing to the ones
who went down in defeat.

About the Photographer

My first real interest in photography came when my children were born. I, like most dads, thought they were the most beautiful children in the world and I began to take pictures of them.

I am an alcoholic who has lived on the street with the men and women you find in these pages. To stay sober, my camera became my sponsor, my reason to continue – one day at a time. I began to capture the life on the streets of the men and women that I have come to know as my family. Their stories are rich, their pain is real, their laughter uplifting.

At first I gave my pictures away to those who I captured on film. Then, the late Jim Samson suggested that we put together a book that would capture in a real way the life on the street. About the same time, Reverend Allen Tysick, a street minister, was collecting in his journal some of the things people from the street were saying to him. Robert de Young was available to review the stories and to work on the text. So together, the men and women of the street, and Reverend Al

and I began the long, hard task of putting together this book. I would have given up several times, but the people of the street would not let this book die. It was often, in fact, the death of a street person that brought new life to this book. This is their book; this is their pain and laughter.

The pictures cannot hope to capture the essence of their lives but offer only glimpses.

Bob Ballantyne